JOHN JAMES AUDUBON

Copyright © 1988, Raintree Publishers Inc.

All rights reserved. No part of this book may be reproduced or utilized in any form or by any means, electronic or mechanical, including photocopying, recording, or by any information storage and retrieval system, without permission in writing from the Publisher. Inquiries should be addressed to Raintree Publishers Inc., 310 W. Wisconsin Avenue, Milwaukee, Wisconsin 53203.

Library of Congress Number: 87-32350

Library of Congress Cataloging in Publication Data

Gleiter, Jan, 1947-
  John J. Audubon.

  (Raintree stories)
  Summary: A biography of one of the first artists to study and paint the birds of the United States.
    1. Audubon, John James, 1785-1851—Juvenile literature. 2. Ornithologists—United States—
—Juvenile literature. [1. Audubon, John James, 1785-1851. 2. Naturalists. 3. Artists] I. Thompson, Kathleen. II. Title.
QL31.A9G55   1988   598′.092′4 [B] [92]   87-32350
ISBN 0-8172-2675-3 (lib. bdg.)
ISBN 0-8172-2679-6 (softcover)

JOHN JAMES AUDUBON

Jan Gleiter and Kathleen Thompson

Illustrated by Yoshi Miyaki

Raintree Childrens Books
Milwaukee

It was an adventure. It was a great and glorious adventure. Art, love, fame, money—they were all part of it. They were all there in his heart and his hopes as he stood on the banks of the Ohio River.

John James Audubon had suffered much in his life. Born the illegitimate son of a French planter in Santo Domingo, he had failed in business. Two of his children had died. He had failed, so far, in his career as an artist.

And now he was setting out with a packet of artists' supplies, a gun, a thirteen-year-old assistant, and not a penny to his name. His goal? To paint a picture of every kind of bird that existed in the entire United States of America.

It's not always easy to be a genius.

Audubon and his assistant, Joseph Mason, got on a flatboat at Cincinnati. They had no money to pay for their passage, so they had agreed to do all the hunting needed to feed the entire crew. Or perhaps Audubon agreed that they would do it and told Joseph Mason later.

At any rate, hunt they did. They would get off the flatboat in the morning and start walking. After a day's hunting, they would go back to the shore and wait for the flatboat to catch up with them. Flatboats aren't very fast.

Their first day out, the man and the boy, with a little help from another passenger, shot thirty partridges, one woodcock, twenty-seven gray squirrels, a barn owl, and a young turkey buzzard. That was for food.

For art, Audubon shot a bay-breasted warbler.

Back at the boat, Audubon did what he had come on the journey to do. He carefully sketched the little bird, using his own particular method.

First, he set up a wooden frame that was marked off in squares by thin wire. Then he used more wire to attach the bird to the frame. He would choose for the bird some position it might have taken in life.

Then Audubon would take a sheet of paper and lightly draw pencil lines the size of the wire squares. Now, he was ready to draw the bird.

As he drew, Audubon constantly checked his accuracy, comparing the squares on his paper with the squares on his frame. He measured every part of the bird with rulers and calipers.

Back and forth from the frame to the paper he would go. These drawings would not be merely pretty pictures. They would be accurate scientific records. Not one spot of color would be added, just to "make the pictures more interesting." To Audubon, there was nothing more interesting than the truth.

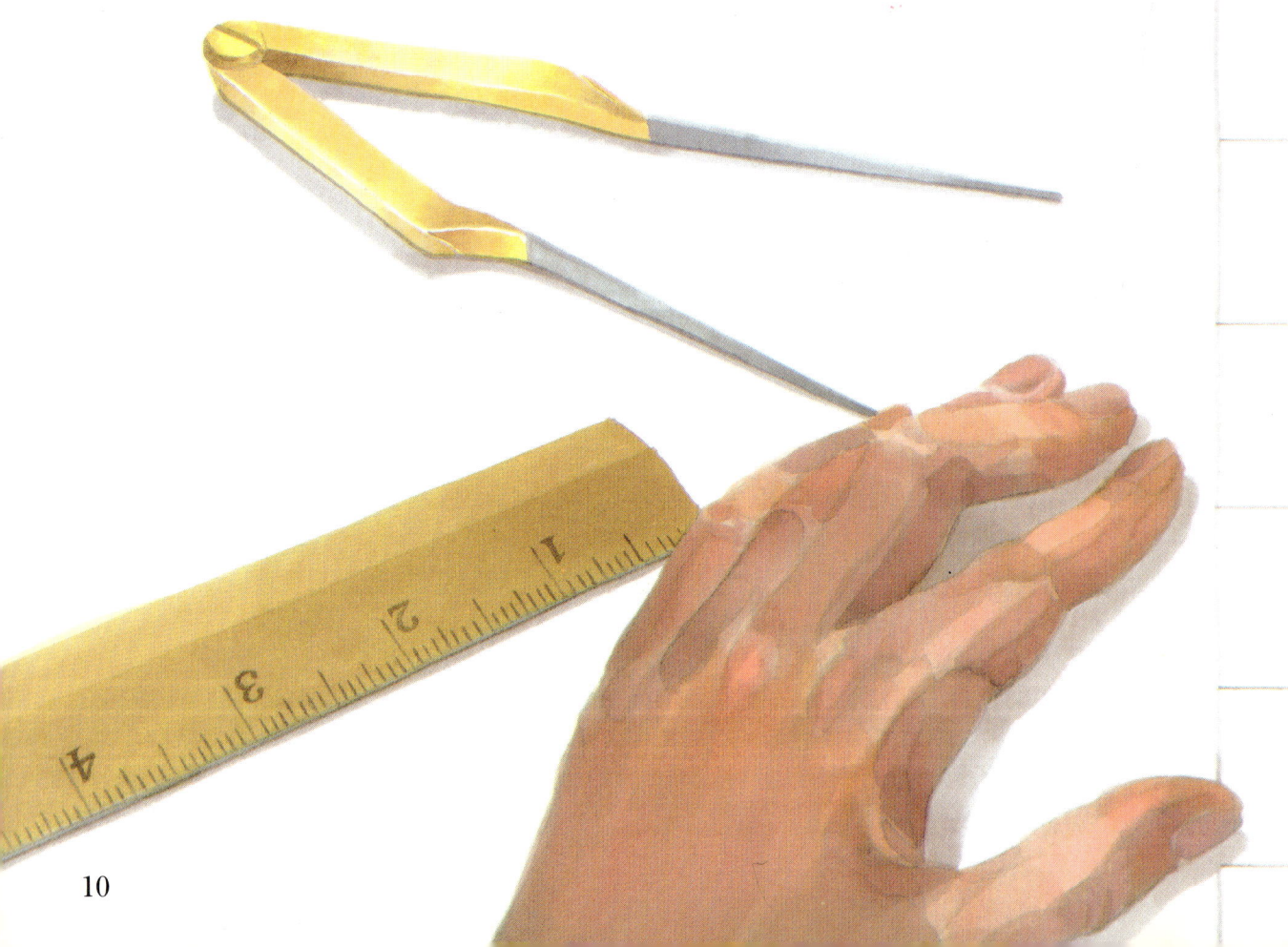

In the meantime, Joseph Mason sat in the corner of the cabin, drawing plants.

Joseph was very young to be away from his family for so long. But Mr. Audubon had offered to teach him how to draw in exchange for his help on the trip. Joseph and his family admired Audubon in spite of his poverty. They decided the trip was a wonderful opportunity for Joseph.

So Joseph hunted birds and worked very hard at his own drawing. He hoped that soon Mr. Audubon would let him draw some of the plant backgrounds for his bird paintings.

Audubon and Joseph collected many birds, but life on the river had its problems. First Audubon got sick, and then Joseph did. The crew of the boat got drunk, argued, and fought. The cook left in the middle of the night, and Joseph had to take over the cooking chores. The flatboat stopped at Henderson, the town where Audubon had failed so miserably in business, and Audubon felt a terrible sadness about his past. The captain made insulting remarks about people who couldn't pay their fare. Audubon took it very hard.

But then Audubon and Joseph got into the forest again. With the captain and one crew member, they left the flatboat to walk to a settlement called Arkansas Post.

On the way, they found a tavern where they got a good meal and beds covered with turkey-feather mattresses. When they woke up, they heard cardinals and meadowlarks singing outside their window.

John James Audubon became really cheerful for the first time since they had left Cincinnati.

It wasn't long after that that they saw the pelicans. It was evening. Audubon was standing on the bow of the boat. Suddenly, there they were. More than a hundred pelicans were resting on a sandbar.

Joseph and Audubon jumped into the small boat they used to get to and from shore. They rowed as quickly and as quietly as they could toward the pelicans.

But before they could reach the large, white birds, all hundred pelicans lifted slowly and quietly into the air and flew away. Audubon went back to the flatboat empty-handed.

Three days later, the captain of the flatboat had a little too much to drink. He started thinking about pelicans. He thought it was a terrible shame that Audubon didn't have a pelican to draw. He thought it was such a terrible shame that something ought to be done about it.

Now, it was raining. It had been raining for three days. It was also ten o'clock at night and dark as ink. But the captain became convinced that he should get Audubon a pelican. He took up his gun and stormed out into the night.

The captain came back sometime later—sober—and without a pelican. A few days later Audubon and Joseph Mason managed to get one.

Just after Christmas, the flatboat reached Natchez, which changed Audubon's fortunes in two ways. The first was for the better.

As he was walking down the street, Audubon met his wife's brother-in-law, Nicholas Berthoud. Now Audubon had always liked Berthoud. And Berthoud had always liked Audubon. So Berthoud offered to take Joseph and Audubon down the river to New Orleans in his own boat.

No more hunting for their supper. No more cooking chores for Joseph. To make things even better, Audubon did some portraits of Natchez citizens and picked up a few dollars.

They set off at one o'clock, on December 30. Berthoud's keelboat was being pulled by the steamboat *Columbus*. Audubon spent the whole afternoon sketching on deck. Then he went down to his cabin and discovered his loss.

A whole portfolio was missing from his luggage. Fifteen completed paintings were gone! Three of them were of birds that no one had ever recorded before!

It was a terrible moment for Audubon. Hours and days of work were lost.

And it seemed as though this bad luck brought more with it. After they reached New Orleans, Audubon and Joseph went out to the market. They ran into a parade and stopped to watch. It was cheerful and colorful and lifted Audubon's spirits. But when it was over, he discovered that his pocket had been picked. There was no money in it, but he lost letters of introduction to some very important people.

Then Audubon tried to find paying work so that he could send money back to his family. And he was turned away by a second-rate portrait artist who would not even let him fill in the backgrounds of his paintings.

But things picked up. People in New Orleans began to hire Audubon to do portraits. The portfolio of drawings was found. And Audubon was hired to teach drawing to a young lady named Eliza Pirrie.

The Pirries lived on a beautiful plantation outside New Orleans. Joseph and Audubon moved out there to live.

Audubon taught Eliza drawing and music, but there was still plenty of time for birds. And there were plenty of birds. The two artists worked hard. By now, Audubon was allowing Joseph to do the backgrounds for his paintings, and Joseph was very proud. Audubon allowed him to write his name in pencil at the bottom of each painting, alongside Audubon's. When they were published, the painter said, they would say, "Plant by Joseph Mason."

One day, Audubon shot two red-topped woodpeckers. But he only wounded them, so he decided to take them back home alive.

The problem was what to do with two live woodpeckers while he and Joseph went on looking for more birds. He decided to put them in his hat. On his head. For the rest of the day, every time he fired his gun, the woodpeckers made a racket in his hat.

When the two artists got home that night, one of the woodpeckers was dead. They put the other in a wooden cage. This was not a smart thing to do with a woodpecker. Within minutes, the bird had pecked his way through the wood and was searching in the bricks of the wall for insects. So Audubon drew him while he pecked.

Audubon and Mason moved on from the plantation to New Orleans, but success still did not come. Joseph Mason had to leave Audubon to go back to his family. He was not yet fifteen, but he worked his way home making portraits of people he met on the way.

Three more hard years passed before John James Audubon had any reason to believe his hopes would come true. And the first signs of success, when they finally came, made their appearance far away in England. There, he found the respect and admiration he had not had in his own country. There, he found people who were willing to help him with the publication of his book. And he found people who would pay in advance to be subscribers—to receive each chapter of the book when it was ready.

Audubon spent several years in England and on the continent of Europe, working on the engravings for the book, making sure that the people who painted in the colors did them exactly as he wanted them, and finding new subscribers.

When Audubon came back to the United States, he did not stop traveling. He had more birds to find.

He went to Florida and collected exotic tropical birds. He went to Maine and Nova Scotia. He went into the wild west of Iowa where he was fired upon by Indians. When it was finally finished, his book contained more than four hundred pictures of the birds of America.

The fifty paintings Joseph Mason did the backgrounds for were included. Joseph's name was not. It's not always easy helping a genius.

SEELIGER SCHOOL